SCHOOL APPEALS EXPLAINED

J. TOMLINSON

CONTENTS

Introduction

INTRODUCTION

Considering whether to appeal after your child has been refused a place at a school can be a daunting prospect for parents if they have not had experience of Admission Appeals before. This book aims to demystify the process so that parents and carers can understand what happens at an Admission Appeal, from what happens on the day itself, to the legislation under which an Appeal is decided, and guidance on how to prepare their case for the Appeal. This book also explains the different sorts of Admission Appeals, as well as the different ways that Admission Appeals can be conducted. This will give parents and carers the confidence to make an informed decision on whether they wish to appeal, and if they do decide to go ahead they will know what to expect on the day as well as the knowledge of how to prepare for their appeal to maximise the chances of winning it. Each chapter has a helpful summary of the information it covers.

There is also an explanation of how places at schools are allocated, and possible reasons why a child may not have got a place at the school requested. This will give parents an understanding of how the allocation process works which will help them in finding the best available schooling option for their child, and be useful knowledge should they decide to Appeal.

Demand for school places is set to increase. Increasing pressure on school places will mean fewer children will be allocated the school that their parents would choose first. This means that the prospect of an Admission Appeal will become more common.

1 WHY DIDN'T MY CHILD GET A PLACE AT THE SCHOOL I ASKED FOR

Summary

All Schools have a certain number of children which they are allowed to accept for each year group. If less children than this apply in the normal admission round then all the children must be offered a place. But if more children apply than are places, not all of the children can be offered a place. The Admission Policy sets out different categories in which children are placed and this is how it is decided which children are offered a place at the school.

If a child is refused a place that they applied for, they have the right to Appeal. This applies to applications for children starting Primary and Secondary School and also for those seeking to change school at other times.

Accepting the place you were offered when you were applying for your child to start Primary or Secondary School, if it is one that you would send your child to means that you have a place secured in case you do not win your Appeal. Accepting the place at this stage does not change your chances of winning your Appeal.

How School Places are allocated

All places at schools have to be allocated using the Admission Authority's Admission Policy. Different Admission Authorities can have different Admission Policies, but there are strict rules to ensure that consultation is done in advance of changes being implemented, and they have to be approved by the Schools Adjudicator before they come into force. An Admission Authority can be the Local Education Authority for Council run schools, or other schools, such as Academies can themselves be the Admission Authority and have their own Admissions Policy. The Law governing this is the School Admissions Code 2012 for admissions up to 2015/16. For admissions in 2016/17 and onwards, the School Admissions Code 2014 applies. The School Admission Code states that all children whose statement of special educational needs (SEN) or Education, Health and Care (EHC) plan names the school must be admitted.

All Admission Authorities must have a Published Admission Number which is the number of children they can admit in each year group.

All Admissions Policies have set categories in which children are placed when they apply for a place. These are called oversubscription criteria and determine how children are ranked and which ones are allocated places at the school if the school is oversubscribed, i.e. there are more children asking for a place than there are places. If the school is not oversubscribed, so there are more places available than requested, all children who applied in the normal admission round must be offered a place at the school. If there are more applications than places, then not all of the children will be offered a place. The Admissions Policy is used by the Admission Authority to determine which children are offered places by being used to rank applications in order against its published oversubscription criteria. The law requires that the highest priority be given to looked after children, and previously looked after children. After children in this category, the oversubscription criteria must then be applied to all other applicants in the order set out in the Admissions Policy.

Different types of school can have different Admissions Policies. One example is faith schools which often give regular church goers a higher priority under their Admissions Policy than non-church goers, or baptised Catholics being given a higher priority than non-baptised Catholics for Catholic faith schools. Some schools ask for additional information from the parent to prove that a child should be placed in a higher criteria, for example a faith school wishing to get further information about a child's church attendance or proof of a child's baptism. If the additional information is not provided, it can mean that the child is placed in a lower criteria than the parents might have expected as the school didn't receive sufficient proof to place them in the higher criteria. This can then mean that the child doesn't get a place at the school due to being placed into a lower criteria than they would have been should the required information been provided at the time of application.

Some often used criteria are listed below:

- Siblings at the School: The Admission Policy must clearly state what is considered as a "sibling" for example older brothers or sisters, half brothers or sisters, step siblings, foster siblings living at the same address, but not other family members such as cousins who live at the same address.
- Distance from the School: The Admission Policy must specify how the distance will be measured- some Authorities use a straight line distance, others use distance by road. The points that the measurement will be taken from must also be specified, for example from the home address to the centre of the main school building. Many Admission Authorities have specialist mapping software which they use to determine the distances.

- Catchment Areas: This criteria is often, but not always used. They must be designed so that they are reasonable and are clearly defined. Parents who live outside the catchment area of a particular school are still able to express a preference for the school.
- Feeder Schools: Some Admission Authorities give priority to children attending a particular school which is named as a Feeder School. This must be clearly stated in the Admission Policy and be reasonable.
- Social and Medical Need: Admissions Authorities using this criteria must set out clearly how they will define this need, and specify what supporting evidence would need to be submitted as proof.
- Nearest school: Some Admission Authorities give a higher priority to children for whom the school is their nearest school. If this is the case it is important to see how this is worded as the exact way in which it is applied can vary between Admission Authorities.

Parents / carers have the right to appeal against the decision of the Admission Authority to refuse admission to their child to the school that they applied for. The Admission Authority must set out the reasons for their decision to refuse admission, and inform of the right of appeal and the Appeal process.

Choice vs Preference

When parents talk about the application they have submitted for their child's school place, they often talk about "choices" they have put down. When Admission Authorities talk about the applications they have received for places at a school, they talk about "preferences".

Choice and Preference are not the same, and it is important to understand the difference between the two in order to have a better understanding of how school Admissions work.

Legally, parents have the right to "express a preference" for a school which is what they do when they name the schools on their application for a school place. For applications to start Reception or Secondary school, the Local Authority co-ordinates the allocation of places and is required to offer parents a place at the highest preference school on their application at which a place is available. If schools are popular and there are more applications than places, not all children will get a place at the school. This means that although sometimes parents believe that if they have put a particular school on an application, they will get a place there because they "chose" it, this is unfortunately not always the case. Instead, Local Authorities have to have regard to parental preferences when allocating places to ensure that the parents are offered a place at their highest preference school, but this does not always guarantee that a place will be offered at a school preferenced by a parent.

The way in which places are allocated to applicants is explained later in this chapter.

Starting Primary or High School

When applying for a place for a child to start Primary or Secondary School, there is a defined application process with key dates. Applying on time or applying late can make the difference between a child getting a place at a school or not.

When the Admission Authority has all the applications in after the closing date, the children are placed in the correct over subscription category as stated in the Admission Policy. The children are then ranked using the oversubscription criteria. If there are more places than children applying for a place, all children would be offered a place. However if a school is oversubscribed (more children applying for places than the Published Admission Number), the Admissions Policy will determine which children are offered places. Starting at the top criteria (looked after children and previously looked after children), all children are offered a place until the places are all used. If there are spaces for some but not all children within a particular category, the children in this category may be ranked such as by distance. For example if some but not all children in the Siblings category would be offered places, it may then be decided on the distance from the school of the child's home, with the places going to the nearest children within that category. Or the allocation could go further down the categories, to children without siblings, who could be ranked on distance. Again, the nearest children within that category would be offered the remaining places if this is how the oversubscription criteria work for the Admission Policy.

If a late application is made after the places have been allocated, that child wouldn't receive a place if all places available had been already allocated as there would be no places left. This can lead to a situation where a child who would have been in a high category such as with a sibling at the school wouldn't be offered a place, despite other children of lower categories being offered places, because their applications were submitted on time. This is why it is so important to make sure applications are done on time. However, this child would be likely to be high up in the waiting list in case a place became available after the initial offers are made (for example if a child moves out of the area, or if they are allocated a place at a higher preference school either through successful appeal or off the waiting list).

If you did not receive a place at the Reception or Secondary School you put first in your preferences, it is very important to decide how you wish to proceed. If you want to Appeal, this gives you a chance of being granted a place at the School via the Appeal process. However, this is not guaranteed, so you need to think about a back-up plan should you not win your Appeal. If you were offered the school you put as a second preference, and this is a school that you would send your child to, you should seriously consider accepting the place. This is very important as it means that you have a place at a school which is acceptable to you even if it was not your first preference. You can ask to be put onto the waiting list for any schools, and if you do decide to Appeal you would automatically be placed onto the waiting list for that school. Children are often offered places through "Topping Up" where if a place becomes available it is offered to the highest child on the waiting list. If this happens to a child who is scheduled for an Appeal for the school that they are being offered, the Appeal would be cancelled.

You do not want to end up in the situation where you didn't accept any of the places offered and then find that you have not been granted the place you appealed for. The reason for this is that there is a lot of movement in terms of school places soon after they are allocated, but by the time the Appeal results are known, most schools will have filled up even if they were not full immediately after the places were offered on the National Offer Day. Waiting until after the outcome of the Appeal is known could mean you no longer have the opportunity to get a place at an alternative school which you might have accepted and there are only very limited options left open to you. If you accept the place that you were offered, this will be cancelled should you gain a place at your preferred school at Appeal.

Accepting the school place makes no difference to your chance of succeeding at your Appeal, and Appeal Panel members understand that accepting a place in this way is a sensible way to make sure your child has a place at an acceptable school while still pursuing your right to Appeal for your preferred school. Local Authorities would advise parents in this situation to accept the place. It is very important if you are going to accept the school place to do this before the deadline stated on your offer letter otherwise the place could be allocated to another child and you would lose the place.

If you would not consider sending your child to the school which you were offered, you need to look at expanding your preferences to include schools you would accept. That way you have the fall back position of a place at a school which you would send your child to with the possibility of still gaining a place at the preferred school either via the waiting list or following the Appeals hearing. If you are in this position, it is advisable to contact your Local Education Authority for advice and details of schools that do have places available. It is important to do this as soon as possible after receiving your initial offer letter to give you the best chance of finding a school that is acceptable to you that does have places available as they do tend to fill up as many parents are doing the same thing. You can also ask to be put onto the waiting list for other schools that don't have places available. There is often movement in school places in the summer term after the offers have been made as even one child turning down a school place, perhaps because they are moving out of the area, can have a ripple effect as that school place being offered to another child off their waiting list frees up a place at another school and so on.

<u>In Year Applications</u>

In Year Applications are where a place is requested at a school out with the normal admission round. This means any requests for a school place other than the usual applications to start Primary or High School. Applying In Year is often if a family has just moved to a new area and need a school there, but can be for other reasons such as if a child is being bullied at a school, or if the parents feel that the school requested would meet their child's needs better.

If a place is requested, in most cases the school should offer a place if there is one available (although in some limited circumstances they can refuse). If the year group requested is full however, a place cannot be offered as the school is not allowed to accept more children than the Pupil Admission Number. If a place becomes available, the place must be offered in line with the Admissions Policy. This means the Admissions Policy must be applied to all the children on the waiting list for a place in that year group to rank the children by the oversubscription criteria, and the place would be offered to the child at the top of the list. It is important to note that a child's place on the waiting list for a school can go down as well as up. If a child who lived closer to the school went on the waiting list, and if distance was one of the oversubscription criteria, that child would be placed higher up the waiting list than a child living further away even if they had been on the waiting list for longer.

2 SCHOOL ADMISSION APPEALS

Summary

School Admission Appeals are hearings where parents can appeal the decision not to be given a place at the school they expressed a preference for. Appeal Panels have the power to grant a place at the school. School Admission Appeals are governed by the School Admission Appeals Code 2012.

There are a number of different people involved in any Appeal hearing.

There is a set decision making process with a number of elements which have to be considered by the Appeal Panel as they make the decision whether to grant or refuse the Appeal.

There are specific timescales which apply to School Admission Appeals.

What is an Admission Appeal?

An Admission Appeal is a hearing where parents / carers of a child who was refused a place at a school that they applied for can ask that the child be granted a place at the school. The Appeal Panel can overturn the decision of the Admission Authority not to offer a child a place, and therefore grant a place at the school for the child. The Appeal Panel is made up of Panel Members who are independent of the Admission Authority and the School. If a parent has applied for a place at a school for their child, they have the right to Appeal if they were refused a place. It is the Appeal Panel that will decide if the Appeal will be upheld (granted) or refused. Their decision is binding upon the school, therefore if the appeal is upheld, the school must admit the child.

The School Admission Appeals Code 2012 states that "Appeal panels must operate according the principles of natural justice. Those most relevant to appeals are:

a). members of the panel must not have a vested interest in the outcome, or any involvement in an earlier stage, of the proceedings;

b). each side must be given the opportunity to state their case without unreasonable interruption; and

c). written material and evidence must have been seen by all parties"

In 2013/14, a total of 50,550 Admission Appeals were lodged by 1st September of that year for a place relating into entry at the start of the academic year. 36,965 of these Appeals went on to be heard. 26.7% of Secondary School Appeals were upheld. For Primary Schools, the overall number of upheld Appeals was 19.6% (Infant classes of which some but not all came under Class Size Legislation had 13.7% of Appeals upheld; Appeals for all other Primary School years had 34% upheld). These figures do not include Appeals lodged in relation to applications for children wishing to move schools within the year are not included in these figures.

Who provides the School Appeal?

For many schools, the Appeal is provided by the Local Education Authority. This means the Appeal is administered by the local Council. Sometimes Academies have their Appeals administered by the Council. For Academies and other schools which are their own admitting authority, they can provide their own Appeals Service which must comply with the same legislative requirements as set out in the School Admission Appeals Code.

The Right to Appeal

If a parent has applied for a place for their child at a school which has been refused, the refusal letter must state the parents' right to Appeal and give details on how to do this including contact details and the deadline for lodging an appeal. Parents must be informed that if they wish to appeal, they must set out their grounds for appeal in writing, and Admission Authorities cannot limit the reasons for which an appeal can be made. The refusal letter must state why the application for a place was refused.

Timescales

Admission Authorities must set a timetable for their Admission Appeals, which has to be published on their website by 28th February every year. This timetable must ensure that:

- The deadline given for lodging an appeal gives the appellants at least 20 school days from the date they were notified that their application for a place was unsuccessful to prepare and submit their written appeal.
- Appellants must receive 10 school days notice of their appeal hearing.
- Reasonable deadlines are given to appellants to submit additional evidence and for admission authorities to submit their evidence to allow the Clerk to provide the required information to the appellants and Appeal Panel so that all parties have a reasonable time to read it before the Appeal hearing.

Admission Appeals must be heard within certain timescales:

- For applications made in the normal admissions round (for children starting primary or high school), appeals must be heard within 40 school days of the deadline given by the Admission Authority for lodging appeals.
- For late applications the appeal should be held within 40 school days of the original deadline if possible, or within 30 school days of the appeal being lodged.
- For in–year appeals, the appeal must be heard within 30 school days of the appeal being lodged with the Admission Authority.

Any appeals which are lodged after the deadline given must still be heard in accordance with the timescales set out by the Admission Authority's published timetable.

Once the Appeal is heard, the law states that letters stating the decision of the Appeal Panel should be sent to appellants within five school days if possible.

Venue

The law states that the venue used for Admission Appeals must be appropriate, accessible to appellants and has suitable waiting areas to allow the appellants and presenting officers to wait separately from the panel before and between appeals. Appeals are often heard in Council buildings such as Town Halls. Other venues often used for Appeals are conference facilities in hotels, village halls (as long as requirements for separate waiting areas are met), or even sometimes at the schools themselves if they have appropriate meeting rooms or offices.

Appeal hearings must be heard in private (except for the first stage of multiple grouped appeals). One party (appellant or presenting officer) must never be left alone with the Appeal Panel without the other. If only one party has attended, the clerk must remain with the Appeal Panel at all times throughout the Appeal Process.

Who is involved in an Admission Appeal

A number of different people are involved in an Admission Appeal:

- Clerk
- Presenting Officer
- Appeal Panel Members

In addition, sometimes the following people can be present, but not always

- School Representative
- Observer
- Legal representative

The appellant might also have the following people if they wish

- Interpreter
- Support person

The Clerk

The Clerk must be independent of the Admission Authority and school. The Clerk must have knowledge of the School Admissions Appeals Code, the School Admissions Code and other law relating to admissions and other relevant law, and be able to offer advice to enable the Appeals Panel to undertake its judicial function. They provide an independent and impartial service. The Clerk is responsible for the smooth running of the appeals process, from scheduling the appeals, appointing the Panel Members who will sit on the Appeal Panel in accordance with the requirements of the School Admissions Appeals Code, sending out the invitation letters and accompanying information to the appellants, collating and sending out evidence to all parties, advising appellants on the appeals process as required, clerking the Appeal hearings, keeping a comprehensive record of the proceedings and writing and sending out the decision letters and accompanying information after the Appeals. They ensure that the Panel Members make their decisions in accordance with the School Admission Appeals Code and provide procedural advice as required. The Clerk also ensures that the Panel Members are appropriately trained before appointing them to form part of an Appeals Panel. The Clerk is the person that the appellants are likely to deal with the most throughout the Appeals process.

Presenting Officer

The Presenting Officer is provided by the Admission Authority to present the reasons as to why the child was refused the place at the school. They answer questions from the appellants and Panel regarding the information they have presented, and also about the Statement of Case that is sent out to parties prior to the Appeal hearing which gives detailed reasons about why an additional child cannot be admitted to the school.

Appeal Panel Members

The Appeal Panel Members are appointed by the Admission Authority, or more usually, the Clerk to the Admission Appeals. They are independent of the Admissions Authority and the school for whom the Appeals are for. The Appeals Panel is usually three members.

The Appeal Panel is comprised of a Chair and two (if the Panel is of three Members) other Panel Members. Panel Members fall into two categories:

- Lay- someone without personal experience in the management of any school or the provision of education in any school (except as a school governor or in another voluntary capacity)
- Education- someone who has experience in education, who is acquainted with educational conditions in the local authority area, or who is the parent of a registered pupil at school.

The Appeal Panel must have one person from each category, plus one more member who can come from either category.

Admission Authorities have to ensure that Panel Members are independent of the Admission Authority and School and retain their independence for the duration of the time that they are serving Panel Members for them.

Some people cannot be members of an Appeal Panel. The Clerk is responsible for ensuring that people who can't be members of an Appeal Panel are not appointed as such. People who cannot serve on an Appeal Panel are disqualified and the reasons for disqualification are:

- A member (Councillor) of the local authority which is the admission authority or in whose area that the school is located;
- A member or former member of the governing body of the school in question;
- Employed by the local authority or governing body of the school in question other than as a teacher or teaching assistant (but those employed as teachers or teaching assistants would not be able to form part of an Appeal Panel for the school that they work);
- Any person who has, or at any time has had, any connection with the authority, school, or any persons as detailed above which could reasonably be taken to raise doubts about that person's ability to act impartially during the Appeals process;
- Any person who has not attended training required by the admission authority arranging the Appeal Panel.

One Panel Member will be the Chair of the Appeal hearings

Chair

The Chair is responsible for ensuring the smooth running of the Appeal hearings. They will introduce all parties present at the start of the hearings, explain the roles of the clerk and panel, explain how the hearing will be conducted and ensure that all parties have the opportunity to present their case to the Panel and ask questions. A good Chair will make sure that appellants understand the process, and feel comfortable to ask should there be something they are not sure about during the hearing. They should also ensure that appellants leave the Appeal hearing feeling that they got the chance to say everything that they wished to, and understood the process.

School Representative

If the Presenting Officer is not from the school that the Appeal is about, sometimes the School will send a representative to the Appeal. Their role is to answer detailed questions from the appellants or Panel about the school if required. If there is a separate Presenting Officer, the School Representative's role is purely to answer questions.

Observer

Sometimes there will be an Observer at an Appeal hearing. This is usually someone learning to do one of the roles involved in an Appeal hearing (e.g. Clerk / Presenting Officer / Panel Member). They play no part in the Appeal hearing or decision making process. Appellants are usually asked prior to the appeal if they mind an observer being present.

Legal Representative

Very occasionally, the Appeal Panel may request a Legal Representative to attend the Appeal to provide them with advice.

Interpreter

If the appellant does not speak English well, many Admission Appeals have the facility to provide an interpreter for the hearing. If this facility is available, there is usually a question on the Appeals Form asking if an interpreter is required, and in which language. Sometimes an appellant will bring along a friend or family member to help them with English.

Support for the Appellant

The appellant can bring along another person with them to support them with the Appeal Hearing. This could be a friend or family member. It could also be a professional such as a Social Worker or Solicitor. The appellant could ask their support person to present their case for them, or just answer questions, or just be there for moral support. Appellants are asked to inform the Admission Authority / Clerk should they intend to be represented at the Appeal Hearing.

What Happens in a School Appeal

The Clerk must notify the appellants of the order of proceedings in advance of the appeal. This usually means that an information leaflet giving details of this, and other information is sent out with the letter notifying appellants of the date and time of their appeal.

For most appeals, the Appeal hearing is done in this order:

- The Presenting Officer presents the case for the admission authority
- The appellants and Appeal Panel question the Presenting Officer about what they have said, and also about information sent out in advance of the appeal
- The appellant presents their case as to why they feel their child should be granted a place at the school that they are appealing for
- The Appeal Panel and presenting officer can ask the appellants about what they have said
- The Presenting Officer sums up their case for the admission authority
- The appellants sum up their case

The Chair would ensure that prior to this, all parties are introduced to each other and that all parties are told that they can ask if they are unsure of anything during the Appeal hearing.

This is the order in which individual Appeals are held. It is varied slightly for grouped multiple Appeals.

Admission Appeals can vary in their duration, but typically between 20 and 40 minutes is allocated for each on depending on if it is a grouped or individual Appeal. You should feel that you got the chance to say everything that you wished to and shouldn't feel rushed.

3 APPEAL TYPES AND METHODS

Summary

There are different types of Admission Appeals:

- Appeals in the normal Admission Round

- In Year Appeals

- Infant Class Size Appeals

- Fair Access Appeals

Different Legislation applies to Infant Class Size Appeals.

Appeals can be done in either of the two methods:

- Individual Appeals

- Grouped Appeals

Types of Admission Appeal

Appeals in the normal Admission Round-

These are for places for children starting Primary or Secondary School so Reception or Year 7. Often run in the Grouped Method due to the volumes concerned.

In Year Appeals

Appeals for places in other year groups, or outwith the normal admission round, for example if a family has moved into an area and the school they wish their children to attend is full in the year group that their child is in. Usually run individually but sometimes can be done using the Grouped Method if there are a number of In Year Appeals scheduled for the same school.

Infant Class Size Appeals

Infant Class Size Legislation applies to Infant classes where the majority of children will reach the age of 5, 6 or 7 during the school year. In practice, this usually means Key Stage 1; Reception, Year 1 and Year 2. This means that except for very limited circumstances, the class sizes are limited to 30 pupils per school teacher. A list of "excepted children"- children who when they are added to a class make it exceed 30 children, can be found in Appendix A.

Sometimes, an Appeal can come under "future Class Size Legislation". This would occur when although the year group that the appeal is for doesn't come under class size, it would fall under this as the cohort moves into a future year group. This tends to happen with schools that have mixed classes with more than one year group of children in them. The Appeal Panel would have to establish if this was the case in deciding the Appeal.

An Infant Class Size appeal is where "an admission authority refuses to admit a child on the grounds that the admission of an additional child would breach the infant class size limit and there are no measures it could take to avoid this without prejudicing the provision of efficient education or efficient use of resources".

The key difference between Infant Class Size Appeals and other Appeals is that the Appeal Panel only has very limited grounds on which they can grant the appeal.

Appeals can be done either individually, or as Multiple Grouped Appeals (usually for large numbers of Appeals for entry into Reception)

Fair Access Appeals

The School Admissions Code requires Local Authorities to have a Fair Access Protocol. These are intended to ensure that, outside the normal admissions round, a place at a suitable school is provided quickly for children without a school place, particularly the most vulnerable children. It also requires Local Authorities to ensure that no one school is required to take a disproportionate number of children with challenging behaviour. In circumstances set out in its Local Authority's Fair Access Protocol, an Admission Authority may refuse to admit a child outside the normal admissions round, even if there are places available in the relevant year group on the grounds that admission of the child would prejudice the provision of efficient education or efficient use of resources at the school. A list of the mandatory Fair Access Protocol categories can be found in Appendix C. Local Authorities can add more categories to their Fair Access Protocol.

If a parent / carer is dissatisfied with the place allocated to them under the Fair Access Protocol, they have the right of Appeal against refusal of a place at the school(s) for which they applied. If the place at the school they applied for was refused despite there being places available in that year group, the Appeal Panel must take into account the requirements set out in the Local Authority's Fair Access Protocol, as well as whether the Presenting Officer has clearly demonstrated that the admission of the child would be prejudicial to the school or other children.

Different Appeal Methods

Individual Appeals

For individual appeals, all appellants have an individual appointment time. They might be part of a day of appeals for the same school / year group, or depending on the size of the Admission Authority, be part of a day of appeals for various schools and year groups. The Clerk would meet the appellants in the waiting area and introduce them to the Presenting Officer (and School Representative if present) before taking all parties into the room where the Appeal is to be held. The Appeal Panel would already be in the room. The Appeal would then be conducted in the order specified above. If there is more than one Appeal in a session for the same school and year group, the Panel cannot decide whether any should be upheld or refused until all of the Appeals have been heard.

Multiple Grouped Appeals

Appeals tend to be done using the Grouped Method when there are a large number of Appeals for one year group at a particular school. This most often occurs for Appeals in the normal Admission Round, i.e. people appealing for places in Reception or Year 7 as they were not offered a place at the school for which they expressed a preference for when applying for their child starting at Primary School or Secondary School.

The Grouped Method is different to the Individual Appeals Method because the Presenting Officer presents the School's case to all the appellants together. All appellants are invited to the Schools Case (Stage 1 hearing) and are also given another appointment time for them to present their case to the Appeal Panel in private. Sometimes the Stage 1 part of the Appeal is held twice to give maximum opportunity for appellants to be able to attend.

The Grouped Method is designed to hear the Appeals in a more efficient way, allowing more Appeals to be heard in one day than if they were done individually. This is because the School's Case is only made once or twice rather than in every Appeal hearing. This allows for a shorter time to be scheduled for each individual Appeal hearing as they will not need to include presenting the School's Case in the hearing. If a school has 80 appeals for its Year 7 intake, this is an important consideration for the efficient running of the Appeals. Another benefit of the Grouped Method is that it allows all the appellants to hear each other's questions and arguments with respect to the School's Case which many appellants feel gives them increased confidence to ask questions and challenge the School's Case.

It is rare, but possible, for an Appeal Panel to dismiss the School's Case at Stage 1 and uphold all of the Appeals without proceeding to Stage 2. If this happened, the Chair would inform all appellants at the Stage 1 hearing. This is unusual, but does happen from time to time. This would only happen if the Appeal Panel determined that the School did not have a Case, and that it would not cause prejudice to the school if all of the children for whom the appeals were for were admitted to the school. If the Appeal Panel found that there were more appellants than they felt could be admitted to the school without causing prejudice, they would have to proceed to Stage 2. This would allow the Appeal Panel to determine which appellants had the strongest cases before granting the number that they felt could be admitted without causing prejudice to the school.

As for Individual Appeals for the same school and year group, the Appeal Panel cannot make any decisions on any of the Appeals until they have all been heard. This means that if an appellant has their Appeal on the first day of a Multiple Grouped Appeal which runs for several days, a decision won't be made on their case for a few days afterwards, so it will take longer for them to find out the outcome of their Appeal.

4 DECISION MAKING PROCESS OF THE APPEAL PANEL

Summary

The Appeal Panel has to follow a specific order in deciding the outcome of an Admission Appeal. The decision making process for an individual Appeal is illustrated in the flowchart. Appeal decisions are made in a two stage process.

Infant Class Size Appeals are dealt with differently, and the Appeal Panel is restricted by legislation which only gives three reasons that allow an Appeal Panel to grant an Appeal.

Admission Appeal Decision Making Process
Individual Appeals

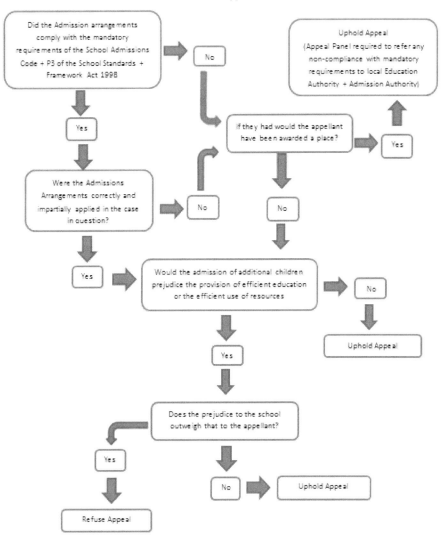

The decision making process followed by the Appeal Panel has two stages.

First Stage- examining the decision to refuse admission to the child

The School Admission Appeals Code 2012 states that the following matters must be considered by the Appeal Panel in relation to each child that is the subject of an appeal:

"a). whether the admission arrangements (including the area's co-ordinated admission arrangements) complied with the mandatory requirements of the School Admissions Code and Part 3 of the School Standards and Framework Act 1998; and

b). whether the admission arrangements were correctly and impartially applied in the case in question."

Compliance with mandatory requirements

Admission Authorities are required to comply with certain requirements in relation to the School Admissions Code in terms of their Admission Arrangements. These include prescribed consultation periods. See Appendix B for full details of the relevant section of the School Admissions Code.

The Admission Authority is required to provide details of how it has complied with the mandatory requirements, and how the admission arrangements and co-ordinated admissions scheme apply to the appellant's application in the evidence that is sent out to all parties in advance of the Appeal.

Correct and impartial application of the admission arrangements

The Admission Authority is required to demonstrate that the admission arrangements were applied correctly in relation to the appellant. Examples of information that could be provided by the Admission Authority to do this include:

If the Appeal Panel "finds that the Admission Arrangements did not comply with admissions law or had not been correctly and impartially applied, and the child would have been offered a place if the arrangements had complied or had been correctly and impartially applied", the Appeal must be upheld. It is important to emphasise that where it is found that the Admissions Arrangements haven't been correctly applied, the Appeal Panel have to be satisfied that the error resulted in the child not being offered a place at the school that they would have been offered had the Admission Arrangements been applied correctly. If they found that there had been a mistake in the application of the Admission Arrangements but that the child wouldn't have been allocated a place if they had been done correctly, they would not be required to uphold the Appeal.

The School Admission Appeals Code then states "that the panel must then decide whether the admission of additional children would prejudice the provision of efficient education or the efficient use of resources". In Admissions, "prejudice" is taken to mean causing detriment to the ability of staff to manage and for children to receive the best education. An additional child being admitted could cause this due to overcrowding, dilution of teacher: staff ratios which reduce the ability and time of staff to support pupils individually and the general erosion of standards at the school because of this.

This means that the school in addition to stating that they have reached their Published Admission Number in the relevant year group (the year group for which the appellant is appealing for a place) has to demonstrate how additional children would cause prejudice to the efficient education or efficient use of resources.

Examples of information that the Admission Authority could provide to demonstrate this could include mentioning overcrowding problems with the physical school facilities, the impact of additional children on staffing resources and the increase in teaching group size. Detailed examples are provided later in this book.

These points make the case of the Admission Authority for the Appeal Hearing.

The School Admission Appeals Code 2012 states that the Appeal Panel must uphold (grant) the appeal at the first stage where:

"a). It finds that the admission arrangements did not comply with admissions law or had not been correctly and impartially applied, and the child would have been offered a place if the arrangements had complied or had been correctly and impartially applied; or

b). it finds that the admission of additional children would not prejudice the provision of efficient education or efficient use of resources"

The only exception to this is for a multiple group of appeals to the same year group (usually for Reception or Year 7 intakes) where if a number of children would have their appeals granted at this point, and to admit that number would seriously prejudice the provision of efficient education or efficient use of resources, the panel is required to proceed to the second stage.

The School Admission Appeals Code 2012 states that the panel must proceed to the second stage where:

"a). it finds that the admission arrangements did comply with admissions law and that they were correctly and impartially applied to the child; or

b) it finds that the admission arrangements did not comply with admissions law or were not correctly and impartially applied but that, if they had complied and had been correctly and impartially applied, the child would not have been offered a place; and it finds that the admission of additional children <u>would</u> prejudice the provision of efficient education or efficient use of resources"

Second stage- balancing the arguments

The next stage of the Appeal is where the appellant states their reasons for wishing their child to be granted a place at the school being appealed for.

The Appeal Panel is required to balance the prejudice to the school (in taking an additional child) against the appellant's case for the child to be admitted to the school (i.e. prejudice to the child if they aren't granted a place). The Panel has to take into consideration the appellant's reasons for expressing a preference for that school, including what that specific school can offer the child that the allocated, or other schools cannot. If the panel considers that the appellant's case outweighs the school's case then it must uphold the appeal.

When considering prejudice, the Admission Authority must be able to demonstrate prejudice over and above the fact that the published admission number has already been reached. The Appeal Panel cannot reassess the capacity of the school, but has to consider the impact on the school of any additional children being admitted. In deciding if there would be prejudice or not, the Appeal Panel may consider the following factors

a). what effect an additional child would have on the school in the current and following academic years as that year group moves up through the school;

b). whether the school's physical accommodation or organisation has had any changes since the admission number was originally set for the relevant year group;

c). the impact of the locally agreed Fair Access Protocol

d). the impact on the organisation and size of classes, the availability of teaching staff and the effect on children already attending the school if an additional child was admitted.

For multiple appeals, the Appeal Panel must not compare the individual cases when deciding if an appellant's case outweighs the prejudice to the school unless it finds that there are more cases which outweigh prejudice than the school can admit, then it will compare the cases and uphold those with the strongest cases for admission. Where a certain number of children could be admitted without causing prejudice, the panel must uphold the appeals of at least that number of children. The Appeal Panel must be consistent in its decision making.

All decisions made by the Appeal Panel are binding on the school. Appeal Panels cannot make decisions with any form of conditions or future requirements (such as if the child attained certain grades or attendance levels), they have to make them at the conclusion of the Appeals being heard in that year group for that school.

___

Class Size Legislation Appeals

Appeals which come under Class Size Legislation are different because the Appeal Panel only has certain set reasons for which it can grant the Appeal to the appellant.

In summary, the only reasons that a Class Size Legislation appeal can be granted are:

- The child would have been offered a place if the admission arrangements had complied with the relevant legislation
- The child would have been offered a place if the admission arrangements had been applied correctly
- The Appeal Panel finds that the decision to refuse admission to the child was not one that a reasonable authority would have made in the circumstances of the case.

The information below is for appeals where an Admission Authority has refused to grant a place to a child on the grounds that the admission of a further child would breach the infant class size limit and there are no measures it could take to avoid this without prejudicing the provision of efficient education or efficient use of resources. Decisions on appeals for infant classes where the refusal was for any other reason are dealt with in the manner outlined above.

As before, the Appeal Panel has to follow a two stage process in making the decision as to whether it will uphold the Appeal.

First stage- examining the decision to refuse admission

The Appeal Panel has to consider all of the points listed below as listed in the School Admission Appeals Code 2012:

"a). whether the admission of an additional child / additional children would breach the infant class size limit;

b). whether the admission arrangements (including the area's co-ordinated admission arrangements) complied with the mandatory requirements of the School Admissions Code and Part 3 of the School Standards and Framework Act 1998;

c). whether the admission arrangements were correctly and impartially applied in the case(s) in question; and

d). whether the decision to refuse admission was one which a reasonable admission authority would have made in the circumstances of the case"

The Appeal Panel is only allowed to uphold the Appeal at this stage where:

"a). It finds that the admission of additional children would not breach the infant class size limit; or

b). it finds that the admission arrangements did not comply with admissions law or were not correctly and impartially applied and the child would have been offered a place if the arrangements had complied or had been correctly and impartially applied; or

c). it decides that the decision to refuse admission was not one which a reasonable admission authority would have made in the circumstances of the case"

The Appeal Panel must refuse the appeal after the first stage if it finds that:

"a). it finds that the admissions arrangements did comply with admissions law and were correctly and impartially applied; or

b). it finds that the admission arrangements did not comply with admissions law or were not correctly or impartially applied, but that, if they had complied and had been correctly and impartially applied, the child would not have been offered a place;

and it finds that the decision to refuse admission was one which a reasonable admission authority could have made"

These are the only grounds on which a Class Size Legislation Appeal can be granted.

Similarly to other appeals, if for multiple appeals, a number of children would have been offered a place following the first stage (such as if the admission arrangements had been done incorrectly), and to admit that number of children would seriously prejudice the provision of efficient education or efficient use of resources, the panel have to go onto the second stage.

Second stage- comparing cases

The Appeal Panel has to compare the appellants' cases for their children to be admitted and decide which to uphold. If the school could admit a certain number of children without breaching the infant class size limit (or without needing to take measures to avoid breaching it that would prejudice the provision of efficient education or efficient use of resources) the panel must uphold the appeals of at least that number of children.

Reasonableness when used in the legislation applying to School Admission Appeals has a specific definition and the threshold is high. For the Appeal Panel to find that the decision was not one that a reasonable authority would make, they need to be satisfied that the decision to refuse to admit the child was "perverse in the light of the admission arrangements" , so "beyond the range of responses open to a reasonable decision maker" or "a decision which is so outrageous in its defiance of logic or of accepted moral standards that no sensible person who had applied his mind to the question could have arrived at it".

5 SO YOU WANT TO APPEAL- WHAT HAPPENS NOW?

Summary

If you have decided you would like to Appeal, you will need to inform the Admission Authority of this. You will then receive a letter notifying you of the date and time of the Appeal.

If asked to in the letter, you should contact the Admission Authority or Clerk to inform them if you will be able to attend the Appeal on the date and time you have been given.

If you can't attend on the date and time given, you may be able to get the Appeal rearranged within the Appeals being held for that school if they are over several days, or you could have it heard without you being there, or you could ask the Admission Authority if it could be arranged for another date although if this is possible it could be quite some time after the original date you were given.

Notifying the Admission Authority that you wish to Appeal

If you have decided that you would like to Appeal, you need to inform the Admission Authority. The letter that informed you that you had not been offered a place at the school should state that you have the right to appeal the decision, and give details of how to lodge an Appeal.

You may have to telephone to ask for an Appeal Form to be sent out to you, or you might be able to download it off their website. The refusal letter should state the deadline for lodging an Appeal.

It is important to submit your Appeal Form within the deadline for these appeals as if you are very late in submitting your Appeal request for Reception and Year 7 in the normal Admission Round, it may not be dealt with until after the Summer Holidays. Although the Admission Authority is required to hold appeals for the normal admission round (Reception / Year 7) that have been lodged by their deadline within 40 school days, the time is measured in school days. This means the time does not include school holidays or weekends, so it can be quite a long time depending on how the Easter holidays fall in relation to the deadline given by the Admission Authority. So if an application is late, although the School Admission Code states that applications should be held within 40 school days of the deadline where possible, or within 30 school days of the appeal being lodged, if it is a very late application it could be that the deadline falls after the Summer Holidays.

You can submit additional information and evidence with your Appeal form if you wish, or submit it once you have been notified of the Appeal date and the deadline for the submission of further information.

Invitation letter

Once you have submitted your Appeal form, it can take a while for all the Appeal applications to be processed by the Admission Authority and for an appeal date to be scheduled. Notification of the Appeal date and time must be provided in writing. Admission Authorities must provide the invitation letter no later than 10 school days before the date of the Appeal.

Parents can waive their right to 10 school days' notice of the hearing if they wish. This can allow their Appeal to be heard more quickly if their application for an Appeal arrives after invitation letters have been sent out for a particular Appeal date which has space for an additional Appeal hearing, or to take advantage of a cancellation.

The invitation letter must provide details of the Appeal date, time and location. It must also provide a deadline by which any additional evidence or information needs to be submitted, and inform appellants that information provided after this date may not be considered at the Appeal hearing. The Admission Authority must also ask appellants if they plan to call any witnesses or be represented at the hearing. If the invitation letter asks you to contact the Admission Authority or Clerk to confirm that you are attending your appeal, it is important to do this.

What if I cannot attend on the given date?

If it is not possible to attend on the date given for the Appeal Hearing, it is important to contact the Clerk to the Appeal to inform them of this as soon as possible. They will be able to give the options available to you. In many cases, the Admission Authority would try to offer an alternative date. For multiple appeals over several days (in the usual admission round) it may be possible to move the Appeal hearing to another of those dates. If it is a single day of Appeals, the Clerk and Admission Authority are likely to be able to defer the Appeal to another, later date, but it is worth bearing in mind that this could be a few weeks later than the original Appeal date given. If the original Appeal date offered is within the required timescales, the Admission Authority has fulfilled its duty in complying with these timescales. In many cases, any Appeals that have been rearranged will be added to another Appeal date that is already scheduled, if there is space, or a day can be scheduled for all the outstanding Appeals heard.

If an appellant prefers, instead of asking that their appeal be deferred, they can either send another person (e.g. friend or family member) to attend and represent them, or they can ask that the Appeal be heard in their absence. When an Appeal is heard in absence, the Appeal Panel uses the written information that the appellant has provided to determine the Appeal outcome. If the appellant wishes to send another person to represent them at the Appeal, they are often asked to confirm this in writing in advance of the Appeal.

If an appellant has previously informed the Clerk that they will be attending, but then fails to turn up for the Appeal hearing, it is common practice to give a small amount of extra time but if they still have not made contact or turned up the Appeal will usually be held in their absence.

6 PREPARING FOR YOUR APPEAL- SUBMITTING EVIDENCE

Summary

The letter that notifies you of your Appeal Hearing date and time should give details of how to submit additional evidence, and the deadline that you need to submit it by.

When thinking about what evidence you may wish to submit, consider why you need your child to go to the school that the Appeal is for. Then think if there is any evidence that you could provide to prove the reasons for wanting your child to go to that school.

It is important to submit the evidence by the deadline given, as this allows it to be circulated to the Appeal Panel members in advance of the Appeal. They can then read it before the Appeal. The Appeal Panel members do not have to accept evidence at the Appeal itself, although they may allow single letters they would be reluctant to accept large quantities of information as it is likely that the Appeal would have to be adjourned to allow them to read it.

Preparing for your Appeal

Once your Appeal date is known, it is a good idea to begin to prepare for the Appeal hearing if you haven't before.

Submitting further evidence

The invitation letter will state the deadline for submitting further evidence in advance of the Appeal. Although many Appeal Panels will accept a small amount of evidence at the hearing itself (such as a single letter) they are allowed to refuse to accept further evidence on the day. This is to prevent appellants submitting large amounts of additional information that would require the Appeal to be adjourned in order for Appeal Panel to read it. This would be detrimental to the smooth running of the Appeals on the day as the subsequent Appeal hearings would then be delayed. Therefore it is advisable to submit any evidence in advance of the Appeal hearing, in time for the deadline given. This is to allow the Clerk to send out all of the evidence relating to each Appeal to all the parties concerned (Presenting Officer and Appeal Panel Members). The Clerk will also send a copy of the Admission Authority's case out to the appellants in advance of the Appeal. Previous legislation stated that this had to be done 7 days in advance of the hearing but this has now been changed to "a reasonable time before the hearing", so all parties should receive all the relevant information far enough ahead of the Appeal date to allow them to read it beforehand.

Think about why you want your child to attend this particular school. If there are any reasons that you could provide evidence for, collect the evidence and send it so that it arrives prior to the deadline.

If you are intending on telling the Appeal Panel that your child should have been given a place but an error on the part of the Admission Authority prevented this, think about what you could provide as evidence. The more evidence that can be given that proves the application was made correctly and on time the stronger your case. It would be much more difficult to convince an Appeal Panel that an error was made by the Admission Authority by losing an application in some way without providing proof that they received it in the first place.

Reason	Possible evidence
Application was done online on time and completed	Screenshots of application process Screenshot / print out of email acknowledging application completed and submitted
Application was sent in by post on time	Recorded delivery / tracking proof that the application was received by the Admission Authority Some Admission Authorities provide a postcard that can be sent out to confirm receipt of application- if this is available this makes excellent evidence of the Admission Authority having received the application and the date that it was received.

Bear in mind that you are asking an Appeal Panel to add a child to a school that is already full, so the more relevant evidence that can help strengthen your case the better. Remember that you are appealing to get into the school for which the Appeal is for, rather than out of the school allocated. This is important as you need to provide a compelling argument as to why your child needs to attend this particular school rather than any others that may have places available. You may have more than one reason to wish your child to attend the school, you can submit evidence if you have it for all of your reasons.

Examples of possible reasons that could be evidenced are given below:

Reason	Possible evidence
Child is being bullied at existing school and this has been reported to the school and or police	Any letters or emails between the appellant and the school which would confirm that bullying had been reported and any other relevant information such as the action taken by the school to address the issue. Letter from police confirming this, with any additional information they are willing to provide. Doctor or other relevant professional's letter stating the effect of the bullying on the child.
Child has a favourite subject that they wish to study for the future and are particularly good at that is not offered at the school at which they have been allocated a place and the school they are appealing for does offer it / has it as a specialist subject	Letter from the current school confirming the child's aptitude and enthusiasm for this particular subject

Child has aptitude for a particular sport that this school offers that the allocated school does not. Perhaps the child is successfully competing in this sport and is considering taking this further in the future with more competitions.	Proof from sport club or other qualified person stating the child's aptitude for the sport and their potential future success if they did have the opportunity to continue with it at this school. Proof that the allocated school doesn't offer this sport.
Allocated school has no direct bus routes so travelling time is excessive, whereas the school appealed for has a direct bus route which would mean the child didn't have to spend x time travelling every day and leaving at x time in the morning / getting home at x time at night at x age, particularly in winter when it is dark. Could also state that child has no friends from their area travelling to that school so they would have to do the journey on their own which would be particularly concerning in the winter months.	Proof of bus routes, for both schools if the comparison between them is relevant to the appellant's case
Affordability of travel to school	If affordability of the child's travel to school is an issue, proof of the costs between the allocated school and the school appealing for could be provided to demonstrate the difference in costs.

Family has just moved house and it is no longer possible for child to attend old school due to the move	Proof that family has moved house- tenancy agreement for new house / final utility bill for last house. If an appellant's case is that they have moved house and are now very close to the school they really need to provide proof that they are now residing at the new address or the Appeal Panel may not take it into account.
Child was living with one parent but this arrangement has now changed and they have moved in with the other parent or family member and attending previous school is no longer possible	Written confirmation of the child's move. Letter from parent who the child lived with previously stating that the child no longer lives with them. Proof that the child benefit if any is being paid to the parent the child now lives with can help provide proof that the move to the other parent is intended to be long term. If there are any issues which might affect the child in relation to the circumstances of the move (such as a relationship breakdown or bereavement), it may be advisable to provide further information and any supporting evidence / letters that relate to this and perhaps demonstrate why this child in particular needs to go to this particular school.

Child or parent have medical conditions which the appellant feels means that they need to attend the school that they are appealing for	Confirmation of the medical condition from doctor or other relevant professional and how it impacts on the child / family resulting in the child needing to attend this school.
Other family members attend the school and the appellant wishes their child to attend the same school for support / childcare / other reasons	Confirmation of the other family members attending the school. Particularly those living in the same house such as step siblings etc.
Relationship breakdown between the child's parents resulting in a need to change school, perhaps due to a house move	Legal documents could be used to confirm this together with proof of the move.
Allocated school does not have an afterschool club or other childcare provision, the school appealed for does and the parent feels that their working hours mean that they have to be able to access the additional childcare at the school	Proof of the appellant's working hours such as letter from their employer stating the hours and also if they would not be willing to change them to accommodate school pick up and drop offs. Proof that the allocated school does not offer the childcare required

Existing Child-minder does not cover the allocated school.	Letter from the existing child-minder. This alone is unlikely to be sufficient to convince the Panel, but if the appellant has found there are no child-minders that will cover the school available and can prove this, that may strengthen their case more than just a letter from the existing child-minder.
Child is a looked after or previously looked after child.	Documents proving that the child is either currently looked after or a previously looked after child. Also if the Admission Authority was informed of this as part of the application, proof that they were provided with this information such as a copy of the application / screenshots.
Child needs to attend this school for religious reasons.	Proof as appropriate to the school. E.g. Letter from vicar confirming church attendance including how long and how often. E.g. Certificate of baptism

Remember that an Appeal Panel has to make a decision using the information and evidence available to it on the day. Supporting information or evidence cannot be provided after the Appeals have concluded as the decisions will have been made. Therefore it needs to be submitted in advance of the hearing. It is at the Appeal Panel's discretion whether they will accept additional evidence at the Appeal itself so to be sure that it can be used it needs to be submitted by the deadline given in the invitation letter.

It is a good idea to have a copy of the information that you have submitted to bring to the Appeal so that you can refer to it if needed.

7 PREPARING FOR YOUR APPEAL- THE ADMISSION AUTHORITY'S CASE

Summary

You will receive the Admission Authority's Case prior to the Appeal. It should arrive early enough so that you get a few days before the Appeal to read it.

The Admission Authority's Case will detail why it was not possible for your child to be allocated a place at the School which you are appealing for. It will also specify how the Admission Arrangements comply with the legislation.

The Case will also state that "the admission of additional children would prejudice the provision of efficient education or the efficient use of resources" and will go on to give reasons for this. Reasons can include overcrowding, reduction in teacher time and increasing of group sizes. The reasons given will vary for each school.

The Admission Authority's Case

A week or so before the Appeal date, you will be sent the Admission Authority's case (sometimes called the Statement Of Case). This document sets out the Admission Authority's case with respect to your Appeal.

Firstly, they will seek to demonstrate that the Admission Arrangements complied with the relevant legislation, and that they were applied correctly to the appellant.

Some examples of what information could be given, either in the information sent out in advance, or in the case made by the Presenting Officer at the Appeal itself are below:

- Details regarding the number of children admitted from each oversubscription criteria together with clarification of the criteria in which the appellant was placed. This could be used to demonstrate that the places were allocated in line with the oversubscription criteria, and that the appellant was refused a place because all places were allocated to children in higher criteria (such as if children with siblings at the school were given a higher criteria, and all places were allocated to children in that and higher criteria, but the appellant did not have a sibling at the school so had a lower criteria).
- The Presenting Officer will often state that the decision not to admit the appellant's child was not personal, and that their application was dealt with in line with their Admissions Policy.
- Cut off distance- this would be relevant in many appeals where distance was used to rank applications as part of the admission arrangements. The cut off distance is the distance that the last child offered a place at the school lives from the school. A cut off distance would be provided and used to demonstrate the correct application of the

admission arrangements by also stating the distance of each appellant from the school. This would demonstrate that the appellant was refused a place at the school because they lived further away than the cut off distance, i.e. that all the places had been allocated to children living closer to the school than the applicant.

- Date of application- if an application for a school place is made after the deadline, it can result in a child who is of a higher oversubscription criteria than others who were allocated a place being refused one. This can happen because when the allocation of places is done, the places are allocated to applicants who have applied by that date in line with the oversubscription criteria. If an application is received after this time, even if the applicant would fall into a higher oversubscription criteria than some of the children who were allocated places, they would not receive a place because they would have all been allocated to on time applications i.e. by the time the application was received there were no places left to allocate. In this type of case, the evidence sent out by the Admission Authority and the Presenting Officer's case would seek to demonstrate how the places were allocated to on time applicants and how there were no places left by the time the appellant's application was made. This is more relevant to appeals in the usual admission round i.e. Reception and Year 7 places.

- Numbers of pupils in the school and relevant year group- this is more relevant to In-year appeals. The Admission Authority would give details of how many children were in the relevant year group, if there had been no spaces available since the appellant had applied for the place due to the numbers reaching or exceeding the Published Admission Number that would show that the Admission Arrangements had been applied correctly as there had not been a place available since the time of application. If a place had been available at any point since the application was made, the Admission Authority would need to show that the Admission Arrangements had been applied correctly in this situation by giving details of the oversubscription criteria of the appellant and the child who had been allocated the place who would, if done correctly, have been in a higher oversubscription criteria.

The Presenting Officer will then try to demonstrate that "the admission of additional children would prejudice the provision of efficient education or the efficient use of resources".

Some examples of what information could be given, either in the information sent out in advance, or in the case made by the Presenting Officer at the Appeal itself are below:

- The school was built many years ago and designed for less children than it has now as the school has expanded over the years. Whilst teaching areas have been added to by converting existing space within the school, and extending the building, the internal corridors remain the same. Because they were designed for less children than the school has currently, there are issues around traffic and congestion in the corridors particularly at lesson change over times. This creates Health and Safety concerns, particularly for the smaller children. Some schools might have implemented a one way system to try to increase safety but the addition of further children to the school would still increase the problems with corridors.
- Toilet provision and changing areas are also often used as examples to demonstrate why the school could not admit any additional children. Sometimes schools have increased their numbers over the years but have not increased toilet or changing room provision, and schools that have converted non-teaching space into additional space have

often used changing rooms resulting in insufficient provision of these facilities.

- The size of classrooms, particularly in newer schools which are designed specifically for no more than 30 children in a class. Some schools have classrooms which only have 30 desks and chairs for each classroom, and there is not room in them to add another set of furniture for an additional child due to the restrictive design of the classrooms. Lack of room and ability to change the layout or classroom design is also a problem that can affect schools in very old buildings, particularly if they are listed as this creates additional limitations to their ability to make changes.

- Children are often grouped in terms of ability, with larger groups for the higher ability children to allow for smaller group sizes for children who need more help, and the provision of one to one teaching support for children with additional needs. The addition of another child would either mean adding to an already large group or increasing the size of the smaller groups, both of which would mean diluting the teaching provision available to existing children at the school. Increasing the number of children would increase the demands on teaching provision, reducing the ability to provide small study groups and one to one teaching support as needed. This would be prejudicial to the children already at the school.

- Additional numbers of children at the school would increase the demand on pastoral support staff, reducing their ability to provide the support needed to children on an individual basis.

- Technical subjects such as chemistry and biology often need smaller group sizes in order for children to be able to do the practical work themselves. Larger group sizes can either mean that children have to share rather than do the work individually which changes the learning experience for both of the children. In some cases, large group sizes can cause Health and Safety issues in relation to space available in the technical rooms, meaning that instead of doing the practical themselves, they have to watch the teacher demonstrate it to them. This could particularly apply for practical work involving flames where it would not be safe to have children doing it if there were too many in the room.

- Other practical subjects such as textiles require teachers to give individual attention to pupils, and their ability to do this is decreased with larger group sizes. Adding further children would exacerbate this.
- ICT is another subject which is often designed to have no more than 30 children in a group. ICT rooms have 30 computers, and the addition of another child would result in two children having to share. This would alter the learning experience for at least one existing child in the year group of the appellant's child should they be admitted.
- Larger group sizes resulting in overcrowding reduce the ability of teaching staff to be flexible in their teaching methods, particularly when rooms are overcrowded and movement is difficult because of this. This, along with the reduction in the teacher's ability to offer individual feedback and support has a detrimental effect on the teaching provision and learning experience.
- Information is often provided about the high level of additional need of existing pupils in the school. This is particularly relevant in the case of In-Year appeals where information can be provided about that year group. There may be a breakdown of the number of children with additional needs in that year group, what particular facilities and teaching methods have to be provided for them and any additional teaching support that is required.

For example if a school has a high number of children with additional needs, they may be providing small group sessions or more individual support which reduces their ability to accommodate further children as the resources are already stretched. If pupils have a teaching assistant with them as support throughout the school day, as well as the impact on the staffing requirements of the school, there is the physical impact of another adult in the classroom, exacerbating any overcrowding issues.

- Presenting Officers will often state that schools are incentivised to take as many children as possible because the more children they have the more funding they receive. However they have to balance this with the ability to continue to deliver the national curriculum to the same high standards as they are currently. The addition of further children would erode these standards due to overcrowding and stretching of resources.

Once you have the Admission Authority's case, try to think about if you can try to disprove it. If you are alleging that an error was made in the allocations process and your child should have been offered a place in the allocation of places, you will need to be able to convince the Appeal Panel that this is the case. Any evidence such as proof of postage / delivery of the application form, print off of confirmation email for an online application need to be brought to the appeal as well as being submitted as part of your additional evidence. This will allow you to refer to them when you are presenting your case.

If you believe that the School does have capacity to accept additional children without causing prejudice to the school, think about why you believe this. Can you provide any proof? Perhaps you know that building work has started at the school which you think will increase their capacity, or that a pupil has just left and another pupil has not been allocated a place at the school. Maybe you have looked at the staffing lists at the school and it appears that there is enough teaching staff to allow for more children to be there. You might be aware that the school has previously had significantly more children than it's Published Admission Number in that year.

The Admission Authority has to comply with reasonable requests from appellants for information which they need to prepare for their appeals, such information could include details of the numbers of children in the year group, the Published Admission Number for that year group, numbers of children admitted into that year in previous years, numbers of children accepted on Appeal in previous years (this does not mean that an Appeal Panel would automatically admit that number again as they do not have quotas, but it could help demonstrate that the school could cope with more children than their Published Admission Number if it has done so before), details of pupil migration i.e. numbers of children leaving and joining the school.

Once you have all the information you need about to the School's Case, it is worth collating it all and making notes on the points you wish to raise at the Appeal hearing, both as questions and as part of making your case. Possible questions that may be useful to ask are detailed below.

Questions to ask the Admission Authority

- What was the criteria and cut off distance for the last child to be allocated a place?
  - If the last child allocated a place was of a lower criteria or the same criteria as your child but further away, you can then ask for further information to clarify the situation such as making sure your child was treated as an on time application if you applied on time. You could provide proof of your application if available.
-

- How many children were accepted into the year group last year? (for Reception or Year 7 appeals).
    o If more than the Published Admission Number- did the school choose to take them or were the extra children a result of successful Appeals? How did they cope with the additional children? If the school chose to take the additional children why are they not taking extra this year? How did they cope with the increased number of children?
- What is pupil movement at the school like- is there a high turnover or little movement?
- Are there any plans to expand the school?
- For in year appeals- what is the maximum number of children that have been in this year group? How did the school cope with that number of children? When did they leave? If they coped with that number of children previously why can't they cope with them now?

The Appeal Panel will also ask the Presenting Officers questions. They are likely to ask for clarification that the admissions arrangements comply with legislation as well as other questions relating to the School's Case. If a Presenting Officer does not have the information to hand to answer the question, the Appeal Panel can adjourn the meeting to allow the Presenting Officer to find out the information. If this happens, you would be asked to leave the room as neither the appellant or the Presenting Officer is allowed to be alone with the Appeal Panel. The Clerk would then ask everyone to come back into the room once the Presenting Officer had the necessary information and the Appeal Hearing could continue.

<u>Summary</u>

Before your Appeal, you should think about why you want / need your child to go to the school which you are appealing for. You will have started to think about this when you were deciding what evidence to submit in advance.

Remember that you are trying to convince the Appeal Panel that your child needs to be given a place in a school which is already full, so your argument needs to be compelling.

Your Case

You need to try your best to convince the Appeal Panel that it would be less prejudicial to the school to have to admit an additional child than it would be prejudicial to your child if they were not allowed a place at the school. Remember you are not appealing to get out of the allocated school as such, you are appealing to convince the Appeal Panel to allow an extra child into a school which is already full when there might be places available in other schools in the area. Therefore the more compelling your case for this particular school, the better your chance of convincing the Appeal Panel.

Sometimes, Presenting Officers will have details of schools in the area with places available in the relevant year group which they will mention in their presentation. This is intended to strengthen the School's case with respect to not adding an extra child to a school which is already full when there are other places available elsewhere. It is worth contacting the Local Education Authority in the day or two before the Appeal to find out what places are available so that if the Presenting Officer makes reference to the schools with places you will have had the chance to formulate arguments as to why those schools are not suitable but the school you are appealing for is.

Think about why you feel your child should attend that school specifically. You will have started to think about this when you were considering what additional evidence to submit but go over it again in case you come up with more reasons and make a list. Possible reasons could include:

-The school you are appealing for is very close to where you live. This would be much more convenient in terms of getting your child to school, perhaps you don't drive and your child would have to walk to school which would be impossible for the allocated school due to it being further away. If you have to walk your child to school perhaps you have other, smaller, children who would struggle to walk that distance twice a day (drop off and pick up-there and back). Perhaps the allocated school is so far away that travel times mean it would be impossible for them to do any after school clubs or socialise with other pupils out of school, but if they attended the school you are appealing for they could access all the clubs and socialise with the other children out of school as many come from the area in which you live. You would be worried about your child being isolated from their local peer group if they couldn't attend the same school as them.

- Why, specifically, does your child need to attend this school in your opinion? Perhaps they are a specialist in a particular subject that your child is gifted in or intends to pursue as a future career. Perhaps your child excels at a particular sport and this school offers far more opportunity to continue with and progress in the sport.

- Does your child have a medical condition that you feel means they need to attend the school you are appealing for? Or perhaps someone who looks after the child has a medical condition that means they need them to attend that school.

- Will all your child's friends be attending the school? Do they have difficulty making new friends? Why would it be better for them to go to a school with their existing friends rather than go to a school where they would need to make new friends?

- Does your childcare depend on your child attending the school you are appealing for? Maybe you have a sharing arrangement with a neighbour or the child minder only picks up from that school or that school offers wrap around childcare but the school you have been allocated does not. Do your working times mean that you would find it very difficult to drop off / pick up from the allocated school?

- Does your child already have a sibling or other family member attending the school you are appealing for? Check the school's Admission Policy for their definition of "sibling". Why do you want them to go to the same school as their sibling? Will the sibling provide support for the child there/ make it easier to get them both to the same school rather than having to get children to different schools / the child that you are appealing for wants to go to school with their sibling or other family member.

- If you have just moved into the area, think about how the move is relevant to your Appeal. Why did you move into the area? Is attending that particular school (if it is near to your home) important to your child in terms of letting them integrate into their local community by making friends nearby? If the house move was due to a relationship breakdown, either between the child's parents or between the child and their other parent how has this affected the child? How would getting them into this school help them deal with this situation?

- Are you wanting to change school because your child has experienced bullying in their last / current school? If in the current school, how severe has it been (give examples), how have the school dealt with it, has it been going on for a long time, has the situation been resolved, how has it affected your child, were the police involved? Maybe you are appealing for Secondary School but you are worried about your child attending the allocated school because you know that children who have been causing your child great distress through bullying will be attending the allocated school but not the one being appealed for.

- If the allocated school is a distance away and involves a significant journey to school, you might be worried about them having to do this journey on their own. Perhaps it involves more than one bus and extended time waiting at bus stops which is a particular worry in winter with the dark nights in terms of your child's safety. You might also have found that your child would

, to leave the house very early and get back late in the
a .ernoon evening because of the travel time involved and you
worry about the impact this would have on them in terms of
tiredness, lack of time to do homework or access any after school
clubs.

- Do you particularly want your child to attend the school you are
attending for religious reasons? Maybe the allocated school is a
faith school. Whatever your reasons, think them through so that
you can give the Appeal Panel full details at the hearing.

Please note that the examples above are purely examples and not
an exhaustive list. You will have your own reasons for wanting
your child to attend the school you are appealing for. It is also
very important to note that it is up to the Appeal Panel to
evaluate the case put forward by each appellant as part of their
decision making process and determine how much weight they
put on different reasons given in balancing the School's and
appellant's cases. Unfortunately there isn't a way to guarantee to
win an Appeal, but the more reasons put forward to strengthen
your case, the better your chance of having your Appeal granted.
The list above is to demonstrate how you might want to think
about the case you wanted to put forward as the more
information you can provide the Appeal Panel on the day, the
better your chance of convincing them that your child should go
to the school you are appealing for.

It is worth writing your reasons down so that you have them to
refer to in the Appeal. There is nothing wrong with having bullet
points or notes with you to remind you of the points you wish to
make, or questions you wish to ask at the Appeal hearing. Many
parents find it very helpful to have written down their key points
and questions beforehand so that they do not worry about
forgetting to say something.

Questions asked by the Appeal Panel and Presenting Officer

The Appeal Panel will ask you questions about what you have said, and the Presenting Officer is also allowed to ask you questions if they wish. Questions often relate to the information you have submitted in advance of the Appeal as well as what you said on the day. Some example questions are listed below to give you an idea of the type of questions that can be asked:

- Following a house move- Why have you moved and is the move intended to be permanent?
- Does your child want to go to the school that you are appealing for? What do they think about this situation?
- Have you visited the school you are appealing for? What did you think?
- Have you visited the school that you have been allocated?
- How would your child get to school? – for the allocated school and the school being appealed for. Is there anyone who could help you with getting your child to school?
- For bullying cases- What has the current school done to address the issues? How successful have they been? If your child moved school do you think the bullying issue would recur again? How would you deal with that and how does the school you want to go to deal with bullying?
- Was this school on your original list of preferences when you did your application for a school place? If not why did you change?
- For late applications- why did you apply after the deadline?
- There are other schools in the area with places available, would you consider any of those?
- What is your back up plan if the Appeal was not granted? (Appeal Panels often ask this, it does not mean they are going to refuse the Appeal, but they are interested to hear what an appellant has to say for this question).

9 THE APPEAL HEARING

The Appeal Hearing

Some points to help with the final preparations for your Appeal hearing:

-The day before your Appeal hearing, make sure you have all your information / notes ready so that you are not worrying about finding them on the day.

-Double check the invitation letter for details of the time and location of your Appeal and make sure that you know how to get there in good time. If your Appeal is being run in the Grouped Method, you should have been given two appointment times (possibly on different dates)

- Take the invitation letter with you so that if there was an unforeseen delay in your journey you could telephone to let the Admission Authority know so that your Appeal was not held in your absence.

- Try to get to the venue a little earlier than your appointment time. This will give you a chance to catch your breath and settle before your Appeal hearing.

Some points to help with the Appeal hearing itself:

- Try not to be too nervous! It is a daunting experience, but all the people involved (Appeal Panel, Clerk, Presenting Officer) will try their best to put you at your ease.

- Sometimes Appeals run late. This can then have a knock on effect on Appeals afterwards. This is frustrating, but not the Clerk or Appeal Panel's fault, it can happen for many reasons. The Clerk should keep you updated and will be working to try to ensure that everyone is heard as soon as possible. Do not worry if your Appeal starts late, it should be conducted in the same way as it would have been if it had started on time and you should not feel rushed.

- If there is anything you don't understand in the Appeal hearing, ask! It is very important that you understand how your Appeal worked and the Panel should be happy for something to be explained to you if you are unsure.

- Try to stay calm. Don't interrupt the Presenting Officer whilst they are presenting their case, you will have the opportunity to ask any questions after they have presented their case and will be able to raise points which you feel are relevant when you are presenting your case. Remember the decision not to offer your child a place was not personal and the Presenting Officer may not have been involved in the allocations process at all.

- Remember the Appeal Panel need to follow their set procedure for deciding on an Appeal so they have to make the decision in the order explained earlier in this book. In the case of Class Size Appeals, it is the law that restricts them in the grounds on which they can uphold an Appeal.

- Sometimes parents get upset at their Appeal hearings. This won't affect your chances of winning your Appeal. Panel Members and the other people involved in the Appeal realise how important the Appeal is. They are used to appellants becoming emotional from time to time and will try to help by perhaps offering a glass of water or if necessary can adjourn the Appeal for a few minutes to allow the appellant to have a break before resuming.

- Try not to worry about forgetting to say something that you wish the Appeal Panel to consider as part of your case. If you have brought a list of your points with you this will help you not to miss anything out. You will have two opportunities to make your case so if you forget to say something when you are asked to tell the Appeal Panel why you feel your child should have a place at the school, you will have another chance at the end when you are asked to sum up your case. The Chair should ask you if you have said everything you wish to before they finish the Appeal Hearing.

10 AFTER THE APPEAL

Summary

You should be given an indication of when you will receive the decision of the Appeal Panel at the Appeal Hearing.

If you won your Appeal, you will need to contact the School to arrange when your child can start there.

If you didn't win your Appeal, you can remain on the Waiting List for a place at the School. You can reapply for a place and have a new Appeal in the next Academic Year, or earlier if you have a significant change of circumstances.

If you feel that your Appeal has not been carried out correctly you can complain to the Local Government Ombudsman or the Education Funding Authority depending on the type of school you were appealing for. Neither of these bodies can change the decision of the Appeal Panel, their role is to review the processes involved and if they feel that maladministration has occurred can recommend that another Appeal be allowed with a different Appeal Panel.

After the Appeal Hearing- finding out the decision

The Chair or Clerk should tell you in the Appeal hearing how and when the Appeal decision will be communicated to you. The Appeals Code states that you must receive the decision in writing, and that the decision letter includes the reasons for the decision that is made. The decision letter must be sent out within five school days of the Appeal hearing finishing. Remember that if your Appeal hearing is early on in a number of days of Appeals, this time scale is from the last day of Appeals so it could be a longer period of time to wait than if your Appeal was part of a single day of Appeals. You should be advised of the approximate date that you can expect your decision letter to arrive. Some Admission Authorities allow appellants to telephone to find out their decision before the letters are sent out, but many do not.

If you won your Appeal- Congratulations and what happens next

If you won your Appeal, your letter should inform you who you need to contact to arrange for your child to start at the School. Depending on if your appeal was an In Year appeal or for starting in Reception or Secondary School, the start date will vary. Sometimes the School's Admissions staff will telephone you to inform you that your Appeal was successful and to make arrangements for your child starting at the school. The Clerk will have informed the Local Education Authority of the outcome of all the Appeals heard.

If you didn't win your Appeal- What happens next

If your Appeal was unsuccessful, you may well be upset and disappointed. Try to stay calm and think about what you want to do next.

Waiting Lists

Your child should still be on the waiting list for the school you have appealed for. Depending on pupil movement, it is still possible that a place might become available. If this happens, the place will be allocated in line with the oversubscription criteria so if your child is at the top of the list when a place becomes available it should be offered to them. It is important to remember though that a place only becomes available when the number of children drops below the Published Admission Number. If a child has left a school but the year group had more than the Published Admission Number, this would not make a place available as the school would still be at or above the Published Admission Number. If a number of Appeals for the school were upheld, this would push the number of children above the Published Admission Number so it could take longer for a place to become available.

Can I appeal again?

You can appeal once every Academic Year. So if you wanted to you could wait and then Appeal again the following year. If you have a major change of circumstances, this can mean that you can have another Appeal earlier. It is up to the Admission Authority to determine what they consider to be a change of circumstances that would qualify for a new Appeal; however examples could include a house move or a sibling being offered a place at the school.

Can I complain?

If you are unhappy about the outcome of your Appeal, you can complain if you feel that the appeals process was done incorrectly in some way.

If your Appeal was for a community, foundation, voluntary aided or voluntary controlled school, you can complain to the Local Government Ombudsman – 0300 061 0614.

If your Appeal was for an Academy, you can complain to the Education Funding Agency – 0370 000 2288.

It is important to note that neither of these organisations have the power to change the Appeal Panel's decision. Their role is to review the way that the Admissions Authority and Appeal Panel dealt with your Appeal to determine if the requirements in terms of administering the Appeal correctly were met, and if the Appeal Panel took the relevant information into account in reaching its decision. If they investigate the case, they will review all of the documentation relating to it (refusal letter, appeal invitation letter, statement of case, the clerk's notes, and decision letter) and can also interview the Clerk and Chair if necessary.

If they do find some evidence of something going wrong in the appeal's process, they can recommend that the Admissions Authority allows you a new Appeal with a different Appeal Panel.

GLOSSARY

Admission Appeal	A hearing that can result in a child being offered a place at the school for which the Appeal is for if the Appeal is upheld.
Admission Authority	The body responsible for setting and applying the school's admission arrangements. For community and voluntary controlled schools, this is the local authority unless it has agreed to delegate responsibility to the governing body. For foundation or voluntary aided schools, this is the governing body of the school. For Academies, this is the Academy Trust.
Admission Arrangements	The overall procedure, practices and oversubscription criteria used in deciding the allocation of school places including any device or means used to determine whether a school place is to be offered.
Admission Number	The number of school places that the Admission Authority must offer in each relevant age group of a school for which it is the Admission Authority. Admission Numbers are part of a school's admission arrangements.

Appellant	The person / people who are Appealing for a place for their child at the school
Catchment area	A geographical area, from which children may be given priority for admission to a specific school. A catchment area is part of a school's admission arrangements.
Co-ordinated admission arrangements	The way in which Local Authorities co-ordinate the distribution of offers of places for schools in their area. All Local Authorities have to co-ordinate the normal admissions round for primary and secondary schools in their area.
Cut off distance	The distance from the school of the address of the last child to be offered a place in the normal admission round.
Education Funding Agency	The organisation who will investigate complaints about Appeals for Academies.
Education, Health and Care Plan	An Education, Health and Care plan is a plan made by the local authority under Section 37 of the Children and Families Act 2014 specifying the special education provision required for that child.

Excepted Child	The School Admissions (Infant Class Sizes) (England) Regulations 2012 allow children to be admitted as exceptions to the infant class size limit. These are detailed in Appendix A
Fair Access Protocol	A protocol that all Local Authorities must have. It has to be agreed with the majority of schools in the area and is meant to ensure that unplaced children, particularly the most vulnerable, outside the normal admission round are offered a school place as soon as possible. The mandatory categories are detailed in Appendix C.
Feeder School	A school named in the Admission Arrangements as one for whose pupils are afforded a priority in the oversubscription criteria.
Grouped (multiple) Appeals	Appeals usually for the normal admission round (Primary or Secondary schools) which are run so that all appellants are invited to hear the Admission Authority's case together, prior to their own individual appointments to present their case to the Appeal Panel. Multiple Appeals for the same school can run for a number of days.

In Year Appeal	An Appeal for a school place outside the normal admission round - not starting Primary or Secondary School but wishing to change schools at a different time or year group.
Infant Class Size Limit	Legislation limits the size of an infant class (a class in which the majority of children will reach the age of five, size or seven during the school year) to 30 pupils per school teacher.
Invitation Letter	The letter notifying the Appellant of their Appeal date and informing of the detailed arrangements such as time and location.
Legislation	Law governing School Admissions and School Admission Appeals.
Local Education Authority	The local councils who are responsible for administering the co-ordinated admission arrangements within their areas for school applications in the normal admission round.
Local Government Ombudsman	An independent, impartial and free service that investigates complaints about maladministration of certain public bodies.

Looked after child (and previously looked after children)	A 'looked after child' is a child who is (a) in the care of a local authority, or (b) being provided with accommodation by a local authority in the exercise of their social services functions (see the definition in Section 22(1) of the Children Act 1989) at the time of making an application to a school. Previously looked after children are children who were looked after, but ceased to be so because they were adopted (or became subject to a child arrangements order or special guardianship order.
National Offer Day	The day each year on which Local Authorities are required to send the offer of a school place to all parents of school pupils in their area. For secondary pupils, offers are sent out on 1st March. For primary pupils offers are sent out on 16th April.
Normal Admissions Round	The period during which parents are invited to express at least three preferences for a place at any state-funded school, in order of preference for children starting Reception or Secondary School. The deadlines for applications are 31st October for secondary school places and 15th January for Primary school places.

Oversubscription Oversubscribed	Where the number of applicants for places is higher than the school's published admission number.
Oversubscription Criteria	The published criteria that the Admission Authority applies when a school has more applications than places available in order to determine which children are offered places.
Prejudice	Being detrimental to something. In the case for Appeals – prejudicial to the school would mean detrimental to the school such as by reducing the standards at the school and the ability of the children already there to gain the best education possible.
Published Admission Number	The number of school places that the Admission Authority must offer in each relevant age group of a school for which it is the Admission Authority. Admission Numbers are part of a school's admission arrangements.
School Days	Days where the School would be open- usually Monday to Friday in term time. Weekends and school holidays do not count as school days. Some timescales within Appeals are measured in School Days.

Schools Adjudicator	A statutory office holder who is independent of but appointed by the Secretary of State. Decides on objections to published admission arrangements.
Statement of Case	The case put forward by the Admission Authority as to why they had to refuse the application for a place at the school and why they cannot admit any further children.
Statement of Special Educational Needs	A Statement of Special Educational Need is a statement made by the local authority under Section 324 of the Education Act 1996 specifying the special educational provision required for that child.
Topping up	This is a term used for the offers of places made to children on the waiting list for a school after the initial allocation of school places. If a place becomes available at a school then it is offered to the highest placed child on the waiting list by "topping up".
Waiting List	The list of children held and maintained by the Admission Authority when the school has allocated all of the places, on which the children are ranked in priority order against the school's published oversubscription criteria.

APPENDIX A

Exceptions to Class Size Legislation

(Section 2.15 of the School Admissions Code 2014)

Infant classes (those where the majority of children will reach the age of 5, 6 or 7 during the school year) must not contain more than 30 pupils with a single school teacher. Additional children may be admitted under limited exceptional circumstances. These children will remain an 'excepted pupil' for the time they are in an infant class or until the class numbers fall back to the current infant class size limit.

The excepted children are: a) children admitted outside the normal admissions round with statements of special educational needs or Education, Health and Care Plans specifying a school;

b) looked after children and previously looked after children admitted outside the normal admissions round;

c) children admitted, after initial allocation of places, because of a procedural error made by the admission authority or local authority in the original application process;

d) children admitted after an independent appeals panel upholds an appeal;

e) children who move into the area outside the normal admissions round for whom there is no other available school within reasonable distance;

f) children of UK service personnel admitted outside the normal admissions round;

g) children whose twin or sibling from a multiple birth is admitted otherwise than as an excepted pupil;

h) children with special educational needs who are normally taught in a special educational needs unit attached to the school, or registered at a special school, who attend some infant classes within the mainstream school.

APPENDIX B

School Admissions Code 2014 - How Admissions Work

"In summary, the process operates as follows:

a) All schools must have admission arrangements that clearly set out how children will be admitted, including the criteria that will be applied if there are more applications than places at the school. Admission arrangements are determined by admission authorities.

b) Admission authorities must set ('determine') admission arrangements annually. Where changes are proposed to admission arrangements, the admission authority must first publicly consult on those arrangements . If no changes are made to admission arrangements, they must be consulted on at least once every 7 years. For admission arrangements for entry in September 2016, consultation must be for a minimum of 8 weeks and must be completed by 1 March 2015. For all subsequent years, consultation must be for a minimum of 6 weeks and must take place between 1 October and 31 January of the school year before those arrangements are to apply. For example: for arrangements which are to apply to applications in 2016 (entry in September 2017), consultation must be completed by 31 January 2016. This consultation period allows parents, other schools, religious authorities and the local community to raise any concerns about proposed admission arrangements.

c) Once all arrangements have been determined, arrangements can be objected to and referred to the Schools Adjudicator. Objections to admission arrangements for entry in September 2016 must be referred to the Adjudicator by 30 June 2015. For all subsequent years, objections must be referred to the Adjudicator by 15 May in the determination year. Any decision of the Adjudicator must be acted on by the admission authority and admission arrangements amended accordingly. The local authority will collate and publish all the admission arrangements in the area in a single composite prospectus.

d) In the normal admissions round parents apply to the local authority in which they live for places at their preferred schools. Parents are able to express a preference for at least three schools. The application can include schools outside the local authority where the child lives: a parent can apply for a place for their child at any state-funded school in any area. If a school is undersubscribed, any parent that applies must be offered a place. When oversubscribed, a school's admission authority must rank applications in order against its published oversubscription criteria and send that list back to the local authority. Published admission arrangements must make clear to parents that a separate application must be made for any transfer from nursery to primary school, and from infant to junior school.

e) All preferences are collated and parents then receive an offer from the local authority at the highest preference school at which a place is available. For secondary schools, the offer is made on or about 1 March (known as National Offer Day) in the year in which the child will be admitted. For primary schools, the offer is made on or about 16 April, in the year in which the child will be admitted.

f) Parents, and in some circumstances children, have the right to appeal against an admission authority's decision to refuse admission. The admission authority must set out the reasons for the decision, that there is a right of appeal and the process for hearing such appeals. The admission authority must establish an independent appeals panel to hear the appeal. The panel will decide whether to uphold or dismiss the appeal. Where a panel upholds the appeal the school is required to admit the child."

APPENDIX C

Mandatory categories of the Fair Access Protocol (from The School Admissions Code 2014)

"The list of children to be included in a Fair Access Protocol is to be agreed with the majority of schools in the area but must, as a minimum, include the following children of compulsory school age who have difficulty securing a school place:

a) children from the criminal justice system or Pupil Referral Units who need to be reintegrated into mainstream education;

b) children who have been out of education for two months or more;

 c) children of Gypsies, Roma, Travellers, refugees and asylum seekers;

d) children who are homeless;

e) children with unsupportive family backgrounds for whom a place has not been sought;

f) children who are carers; and

 g) children with special educational needs, disabilities or medical conditions (but without a statement or Education, Health and Care Plan). "

ABOUT THE AUTHOR

The author has extensive experience working in School Appeals, from clerking individual School Appeals to being responsible for the overall running and co-ordination of the School Appeals Service of a large Local Authority. The author now runs their own Admission Appeal Clerking Service and is also an experienced Independent Admission Appeals Member.

* Look at school's response
* see pg. 54 - 55
* Provide prove that application
  was submitted ontime
  see pg 60 -
* Find out if school
  will be expanded.
* Look at schools closeby
  & state why schools
  maybe unsuitable Pg. 63
* Building case why
  Child should attend
  School Pg.65
* Reasons: bullet points
* Mention preferential list